STEM ADVENTURES

THE DYNAMIC WORLD OF DRONES

MAX AXIOM
STEM ADVENTURES

by Nikole Brooks Bethea

illustrated by Pixelpop Studios

CAPSTONE PRESS
a capstone imprint

Graphic Library is published by Capstone Press,
1710 Roe Crest Drive, North Mankato, Minnesota 56003
www.mycapstone.com

Library of Congress Cataloging-in-Publication Data
Names: Bethea, Nikole Brooks, author.
Title: The dynamic world of drones / by Nikole Brooks Bethea.
Description: North Mankato, Minnesota : Capstone Press, [2018] | Series:
Graphic library. STEM adventures | Series: Max Axiom STEM adventures |
Audience: Age 8-14. | Audience: Grade 4 to 6. | Includes bibliographical
references and index.
Identifiers: LCCN 2017008333| ISBN 9781515773900 (library binding) | ISBN
9781515773962 (paperback) | ISBN 9781515773986 (ebook PDF)
Subjects: LCSH: Drone aircraft—Juvenile literature. | Drone aircraft—Comic
books, strips, etc. | Graphic novels.
Classification: LCC TL685.35 .B48 2018 | DDC 629.133/39—dc23
LC record available at https://lccn.loc.gov/2017008333

Designer
Steve Mead

Cover Artist
Pixelpop Studios

Colorist
TOMMY ADI HUTOMO

Media Researcher
Wanda Winch

Production Specialist
Steve Walker

Editor
Mari Bolte

Printed in the United States of America.
010364F17

TABLE OF CONTENTS

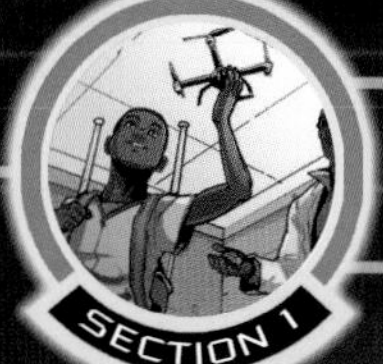
SECTION 1

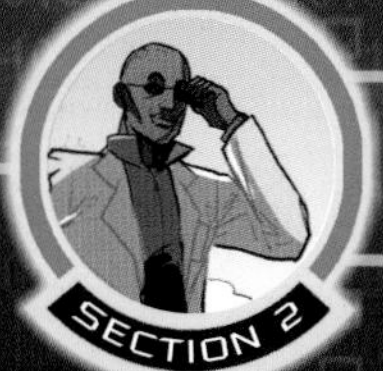
SECTION 2

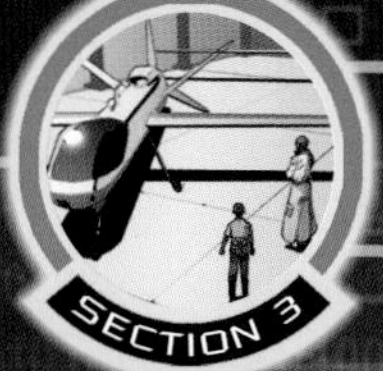
SECTION 3

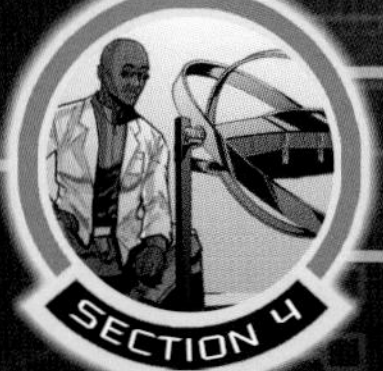
SECTION 4

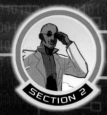

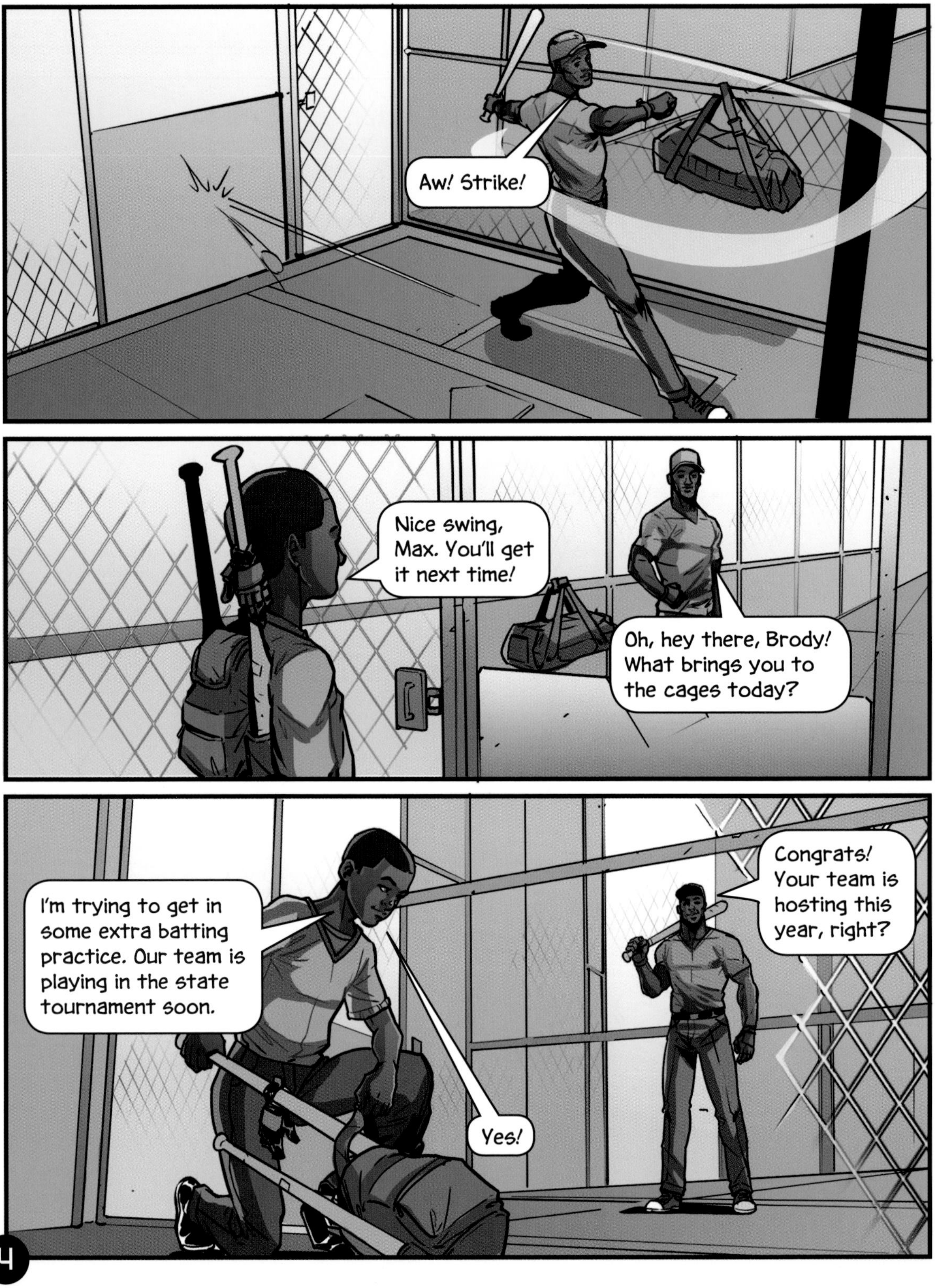
Aw! Strike!
Nice swing, Max. You'll get it next time!
Oh, hey there, Brody! What brings you to the cages today?
I'm trying to get in some extra batting practice. Our team is playing in the state tournament soon.
Congrats! Your team is hosting this year, right?
Yes!

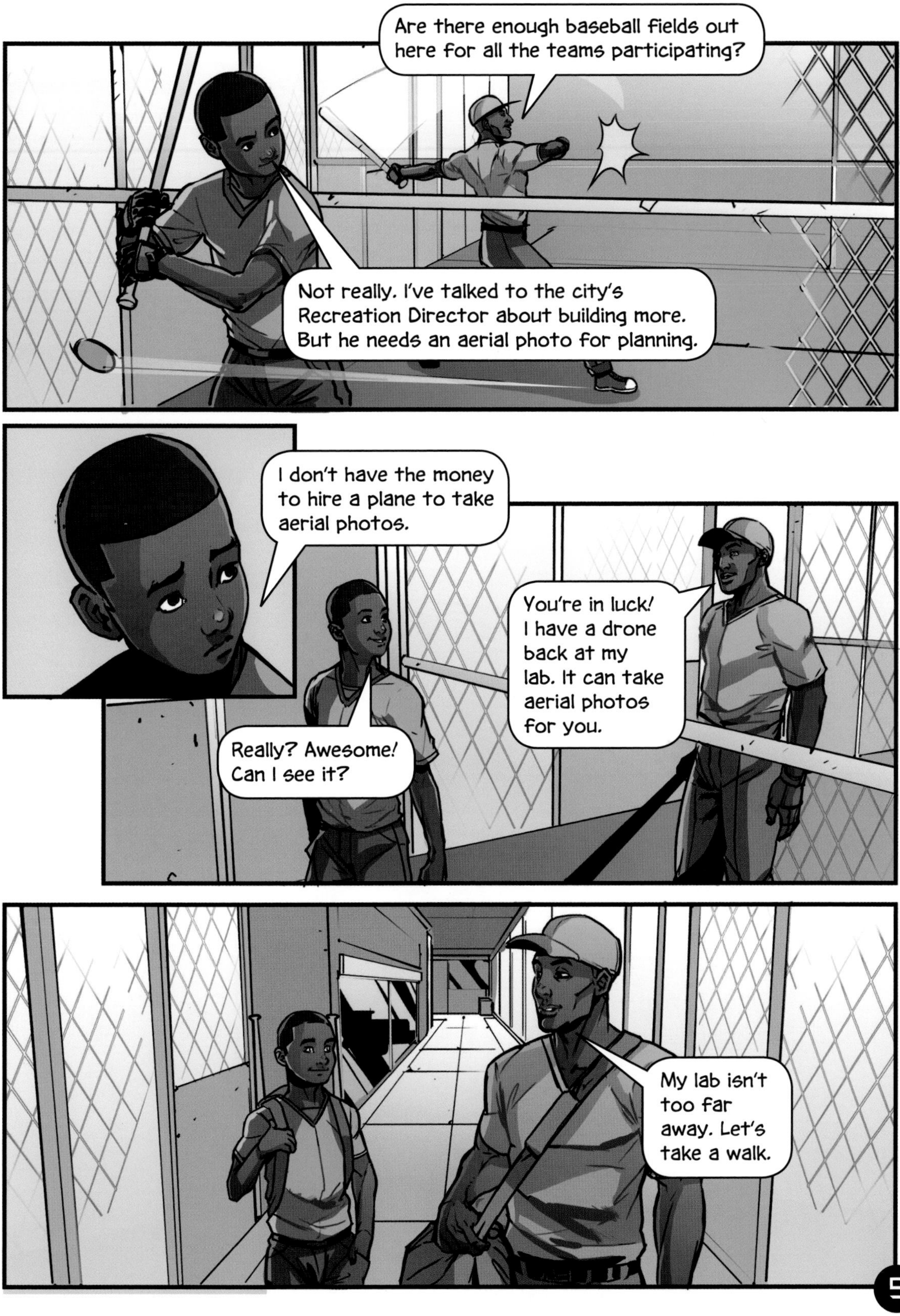
Are there enough baseball fields out here for all the teams participating?
Not really. I've talked to the city's Recreation Director about building more. But he needs an aerial photo for planning.
I don't have the money to hire a plane to take aerial photos.
You're in luck! I have a drone back at my lab. It can take aerial photos for you.
Really? Awesome! Can I see it?
My lab isn't too far away. Let's take a walk.

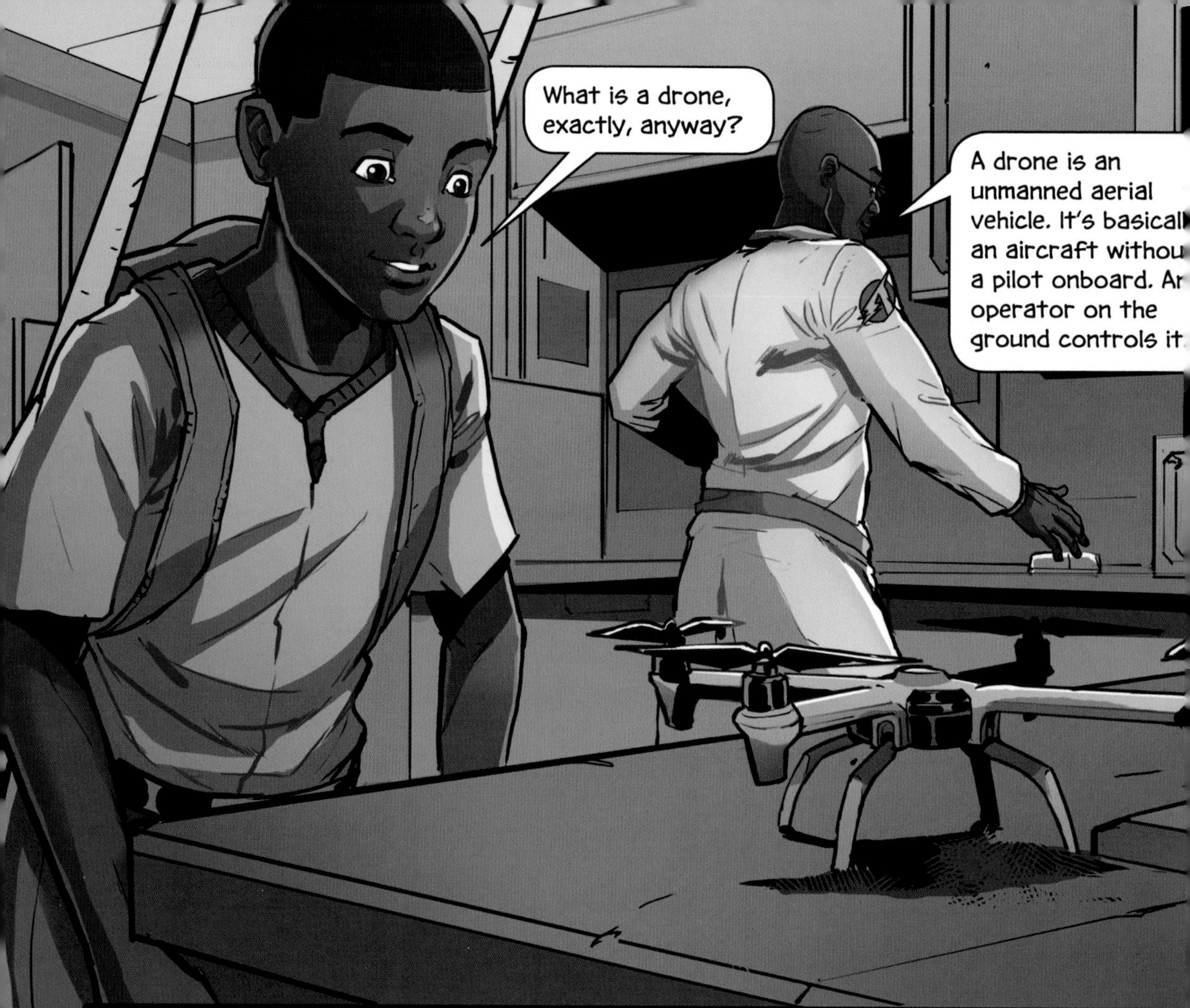
What is a drone, exactly, anyway?
A drone is an unmanned aerial vehicle. It's basicall
an aircraft withou
a pilot onboard. A
operator on the ground controls it

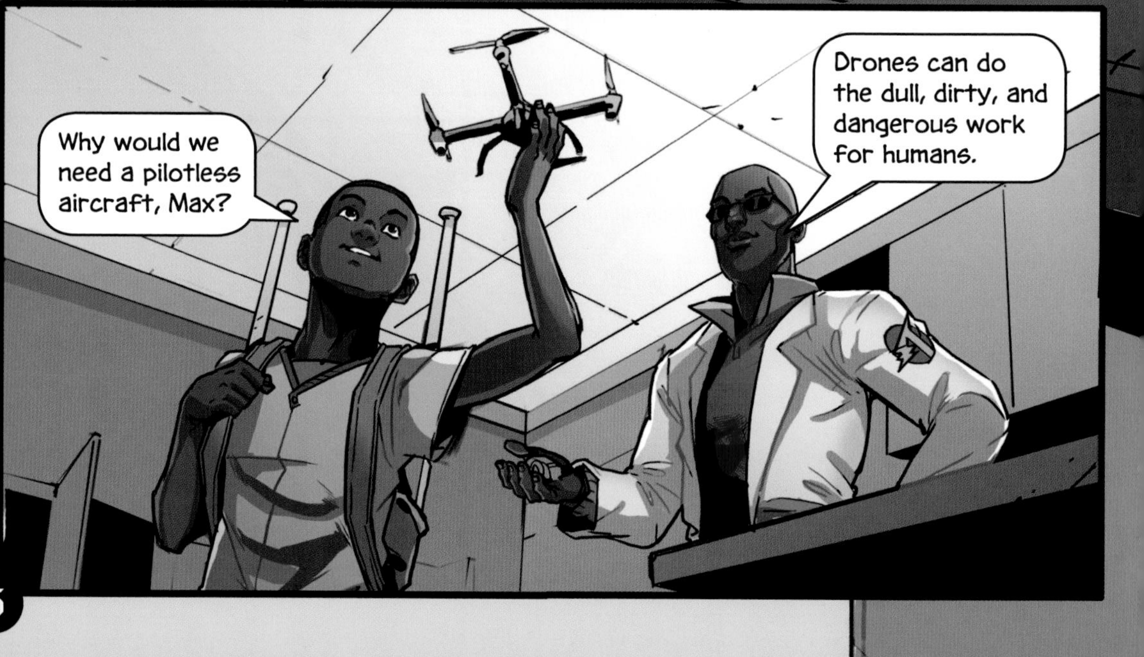
Why would we need a pilotless aircraft, Max?
Drones can do the dull, dirty, and dangerous work for humans.

I'm mounting the camera now. My drone also has a global positioning system, or GPS. This allows me to track its location.

My drone is a quadcopter. It's classified as a rotary drone because of these rotating blades. They provide lift and allow the drone to hover or move in any direction.

Instead of one blade like a helicopter, it has four. Is that why it's called a quadcopter?

You got it!

Are all drones like yours?

No, drones range from the size of a small bird to a jumbo jet.

Some drones are fixed wing drones, like the one shown here in this magazine. They have a solid wing across the top of their body and fly in a continuous forward motion. Fixed wing drones can't hover like rotary drones. They also must be launched into the air.

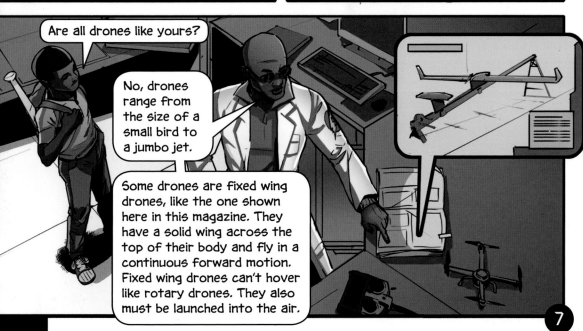

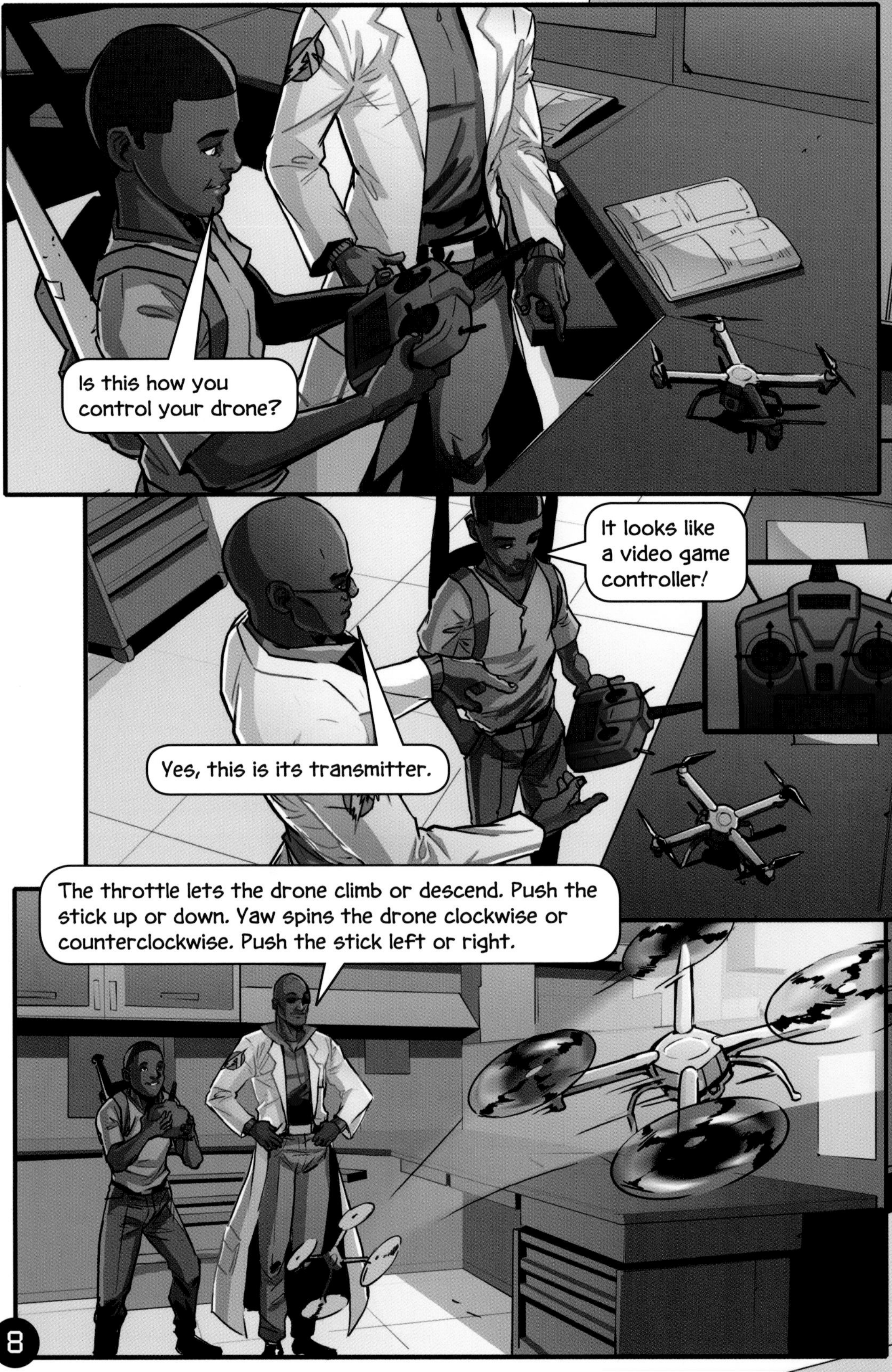
Is this how you control your drone?
It looks like a video game controller!
Yes, this is its transmitter.
The throttle lets the drone climb or descend. Push the stick up or down. Yaw spins the drone clockwise or counterclockwise. Push the stick left or right.

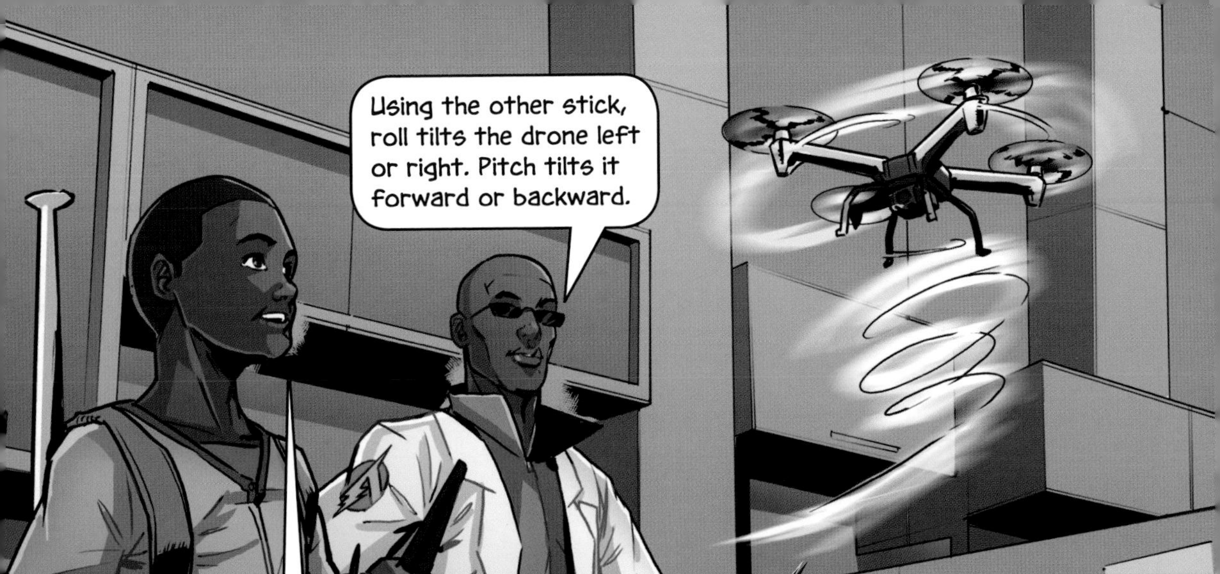
Using the other stick, roll tilts the drone left or right. Pitch tilts it forward or backward.
Wow, this will take some practice and coordination!

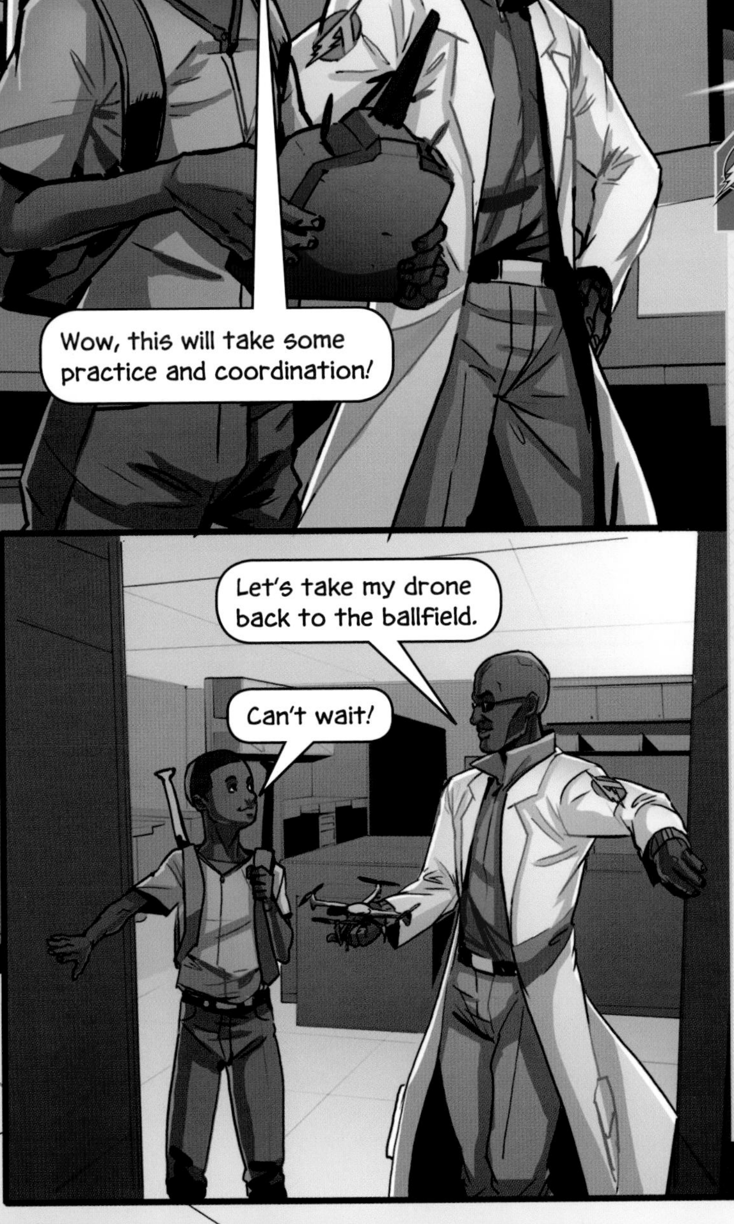
Let's take my drone back to the ballfield.
Can't wait!

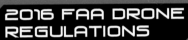

2016 FAA DRONE REGULATIONS

In 2016, the Federal Aviation Administration (FAA) set the following new rules for operating small unmanned aerial vehicles. These rules are to protect manned aircraft flying in the airspace.

- Drones must weigh less than 55 pounds (25 kilograms).
- The drone must remain within sight of the controller at all times.
- Drones can only be operated during daylight.
- Drones can't be operated over people or under covered structures.
- The maximum height drones can fly above ground is 400 feet (122 meters).

SECTION 2 COMMERCIAL AND SCIENTIFIC DRONES

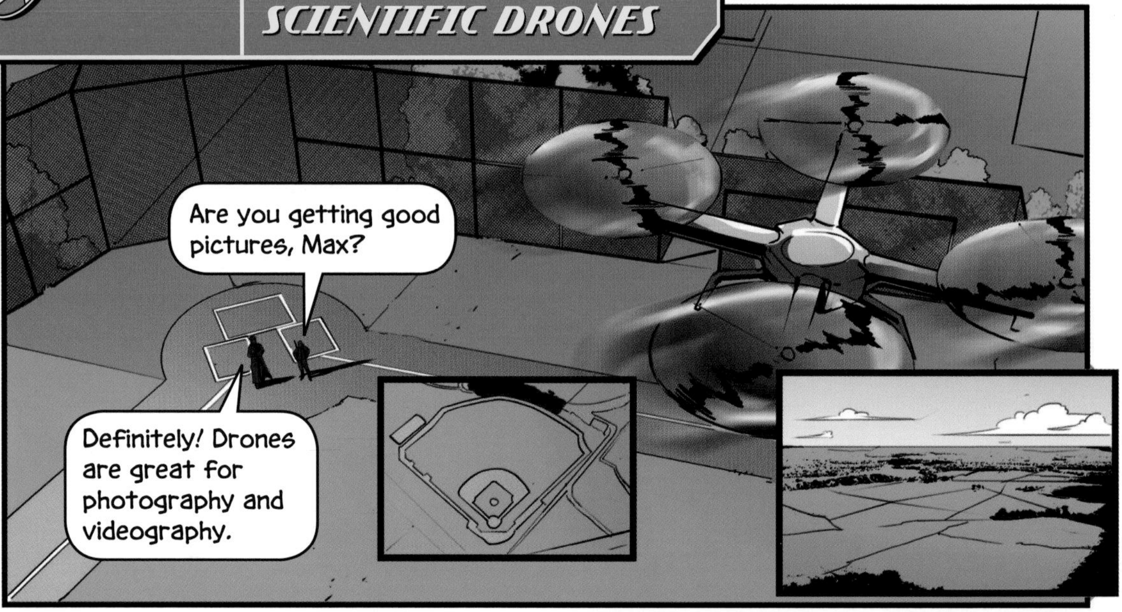
Are you getting good pictures, Max?
Definitely! Drones are great for photography and videography.

FOREST FIRES

Drones can fly over forest fires and send back real-time images of the fire's path. They can fly through smoky conditions that would be dangerous for helicopter pilots. However, civilians should never fly their own drones in the restricted airspace around forest fires. Their drones can interfere with firefighting aircraft, grounding helicopters and even endangering the lives of the pilots.

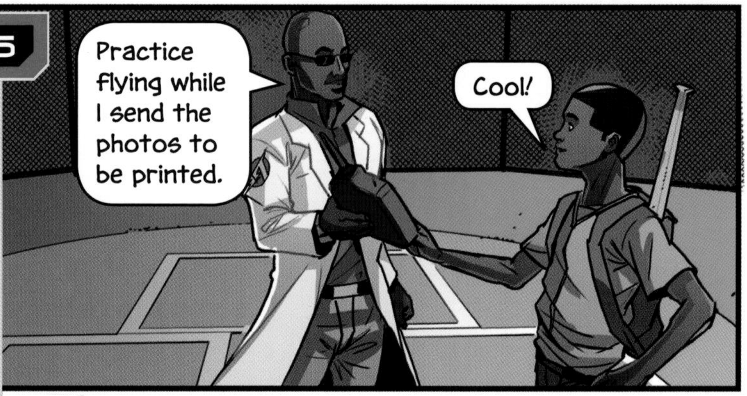
Practice flying while I send the photos to be printed.
Cool!

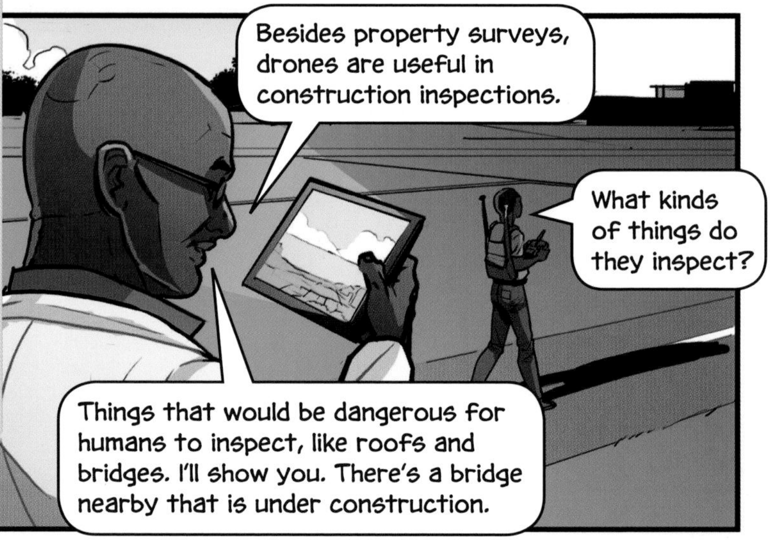
Besides property surveys, drones are useful in construction inspections.
What kinds of things do they inspect?
Things that would be dangerous for humans to inspect, like roofs and bridges. I'll show you. There's a bridge nearby that is under construction.

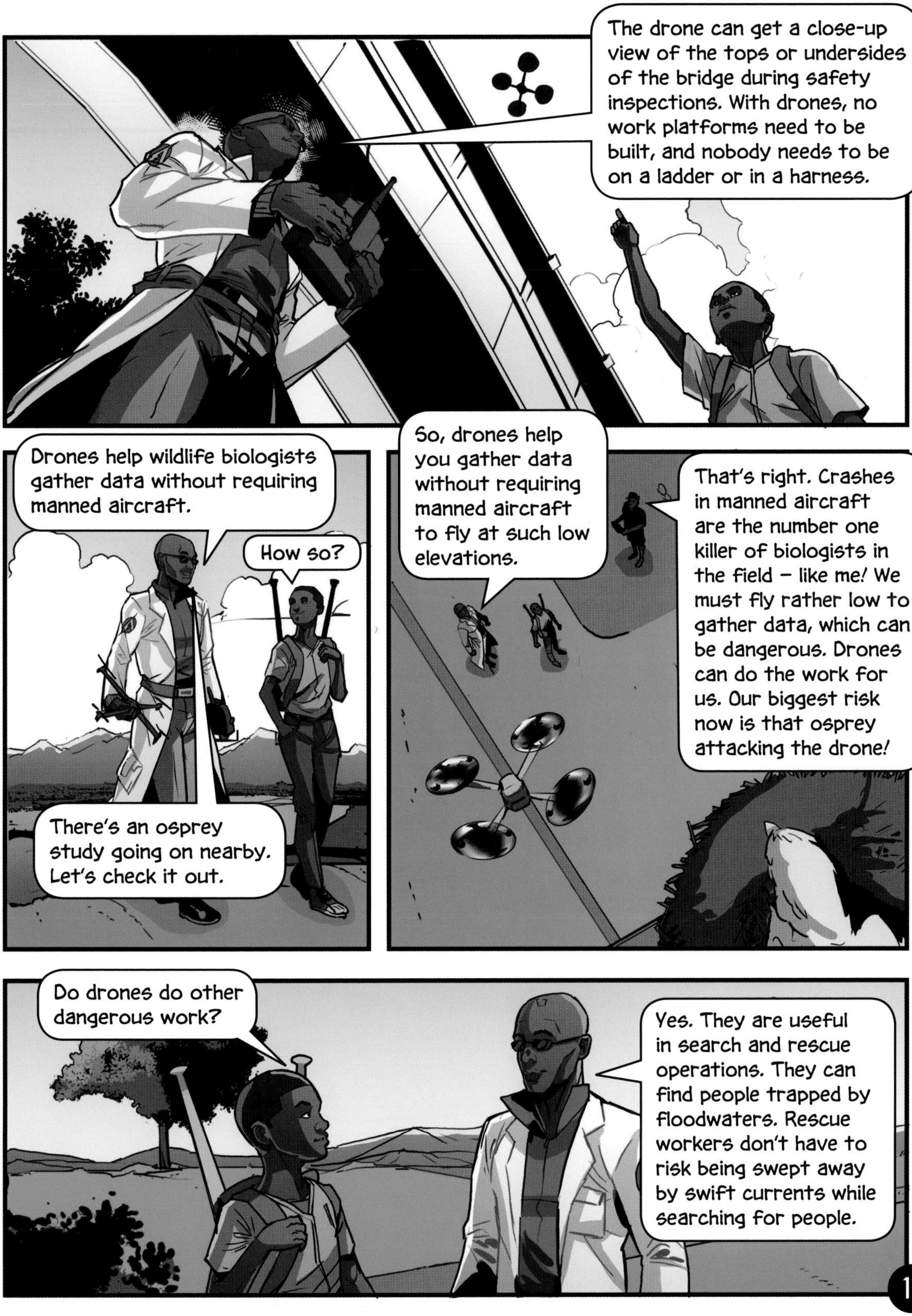

The drone can get a close-up view of the tops or undersides of the bridge during safety inspections. With drones, no work platforms need to be built, and nobody needs to be on a ladder or in a harness.
Drones help wildlife biologists gather data without requiring manned aircraft.
How so?
There's an osprey study going on nearby. Let's check it out.
So, drones help you gather data without requiring manned aircraft to fly at such low elevations.
That's right. Crashes in manned aircraft are the number one killer of biologists in the field – like me! We must fly rather low to gather data, which can be dangerous. Drones can do the work for us. Our biggest risk now is that osprey attacking the drone!
Do drones do other dangerous work?
Yes. They are useful in search and rescue operations. They can find people trapped by floodwaters. Rescue workers don't have to risk being swept away by swift currents while searching for people.

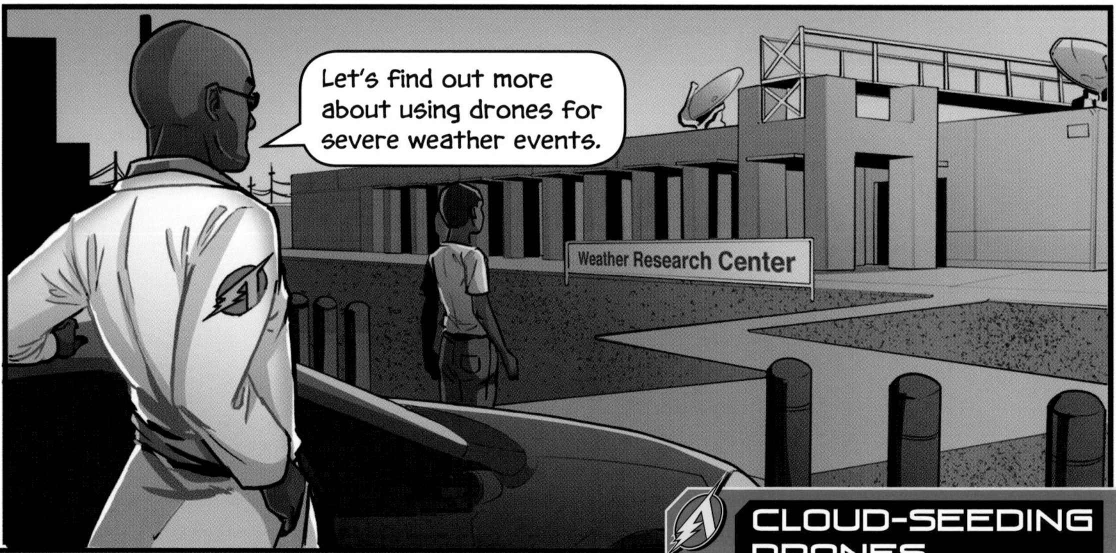
Let's find out more about using drones for severe weather events.
Weather Research Center

CLOUD-SEEDING DRONES

Researchers have been using drones to actually create rain! Cloud-seeding drones fly through clouds and spray tiny silver iodide particles. Water in the cloud condenses around the particles and forms ice crystals. These ice crystals become too heavy to remain suspended in the cloud. They fall to the ground, often melting and forming rain.

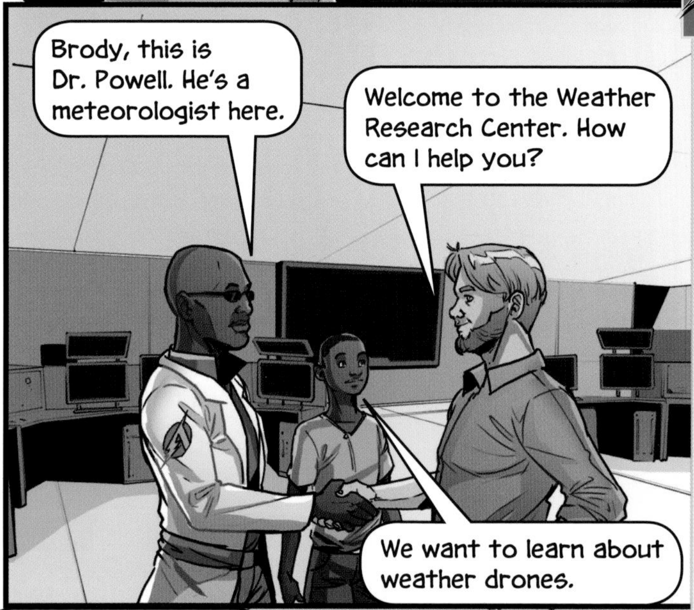
Brody, this is Dr. Powell. He's a meteorologist here.
Welcome to the Weather Research Center. How can I help you?
We want to learn about weather drones.

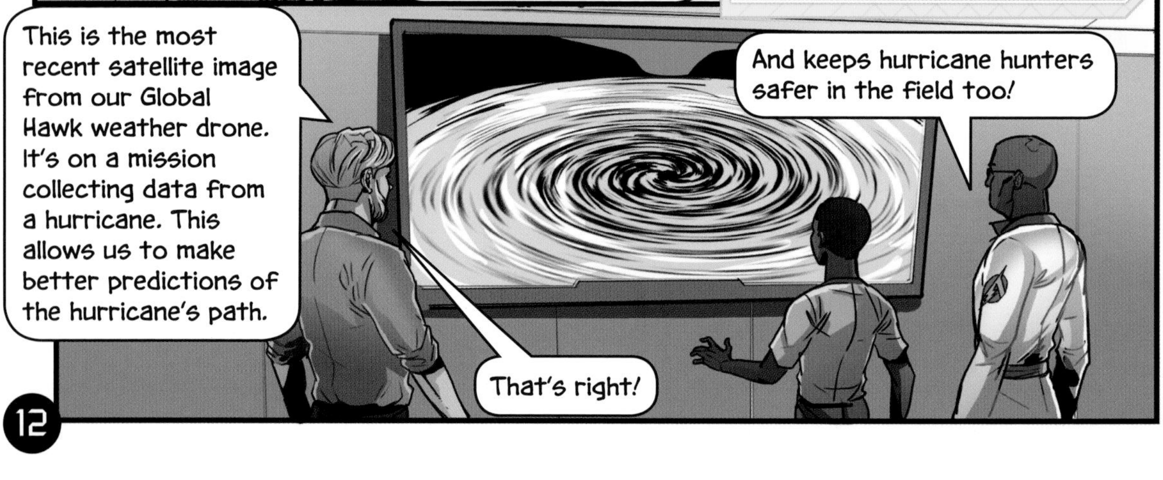
This is the most recent satellite image from our Global Hawk weather drone. It's on a mission collecting data from a hurricane. This allows us to make better predictions of the hurricane's path.
That's right!
And keeps hurricane hunters safer in the field too!

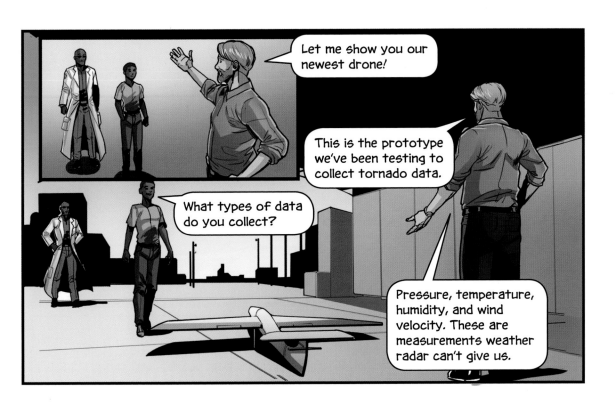

Let me show you our newest drone!

This is the prototype we've been testing to collect tornado data.

What types of data do you collect?

Pressure, temperature, humidity, and wind velocity. These are measurements weather radar can't give us.

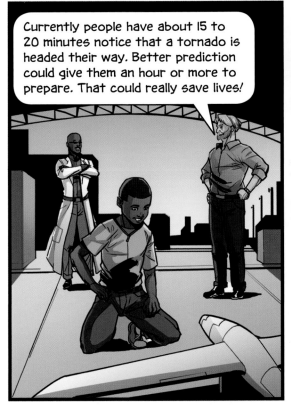

Currently people have about 15 to 20 minutes notice that a tornado is headed their way. Better prediction could give them an hour or more to prepare. That could really save lives!

All this new drone technology seems really helpful!

And that's just the start. Other scientists have been using drones in agriculture.

Thanks, Dr. Powell. We'll check out the agricultural drones too.

Wow! I want a closer view of that!

Hi folks! I'm Jeff Ricks, the agricultural manager.

Is that drone watering the grapevines?

Yes, it's a helicopter drone. We save water by only irrigating where it's needed.

What's that one doing?

That one's a quadcopter. It's taking pictures of the crops.

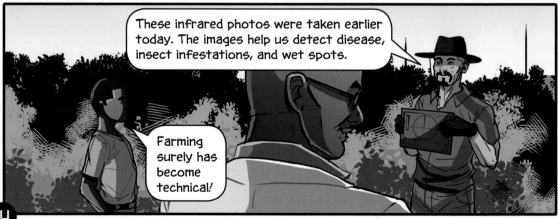

These infrared photos were taken earlier today. The images help us detect disease, insect infestations, and wet spots.

Farming surely has become technical!

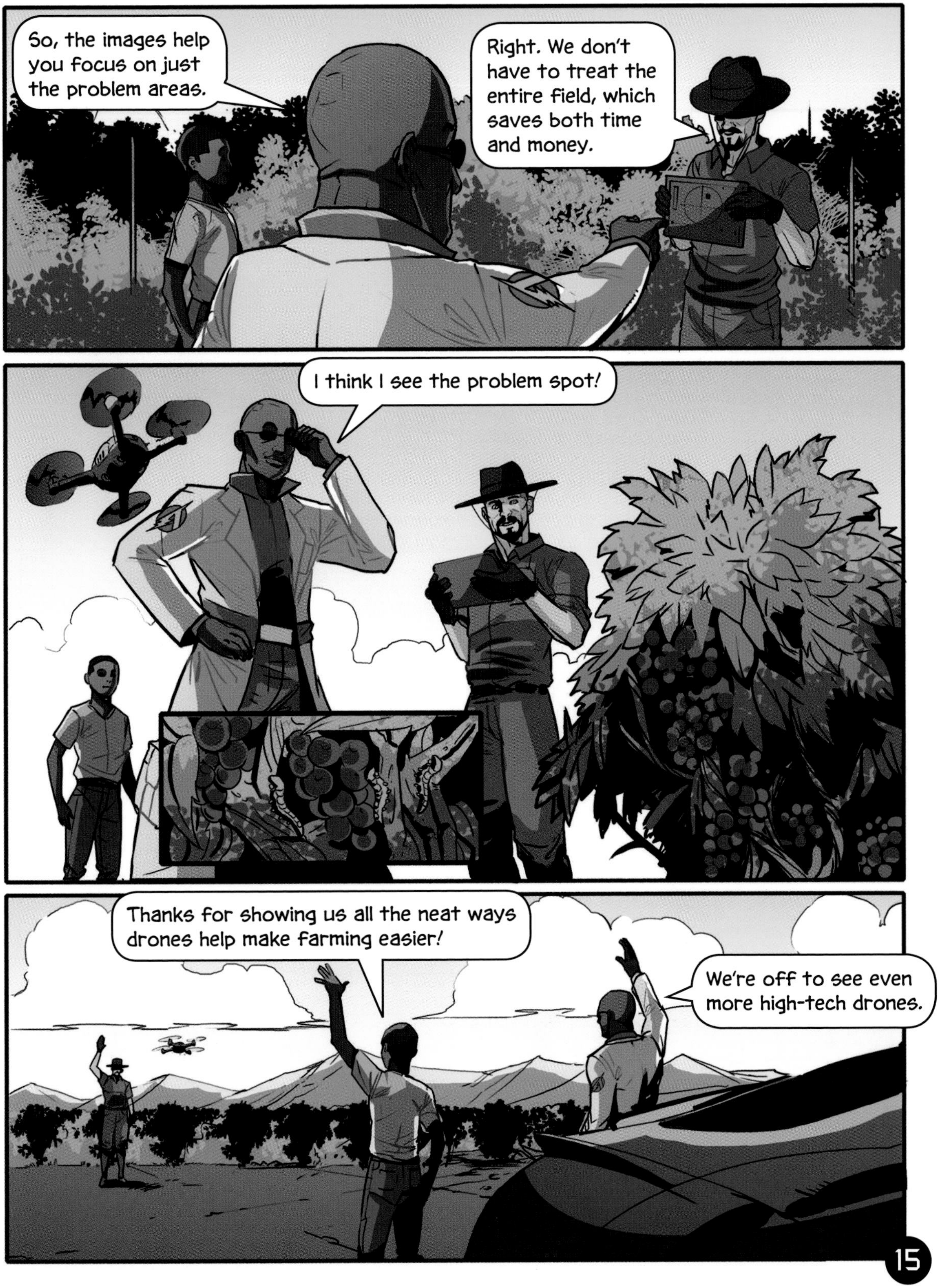
So, the images help you focus on just the problem areas.
Right. We don't have to treat the entire field, which saves both time and money.
I think I see the problem spot!
Thanks for showing us all the neat ways drones help make farming easier!
We're off to see even more high-tech drones.

This is so cool, Captain Russell! Look at all the different drones! What are you holding?

This tiny drone is a Nano Hummingbird. We use it for reconnaissance.

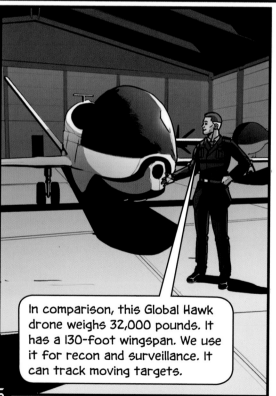

In comparison, this Global Hawk drone weighs 32,000 pounds. It has a 130-foot wingspan. We use it for recon and surveillance. It can track moving targets.

The Raven is only 4 pounds and can be launched by hand.

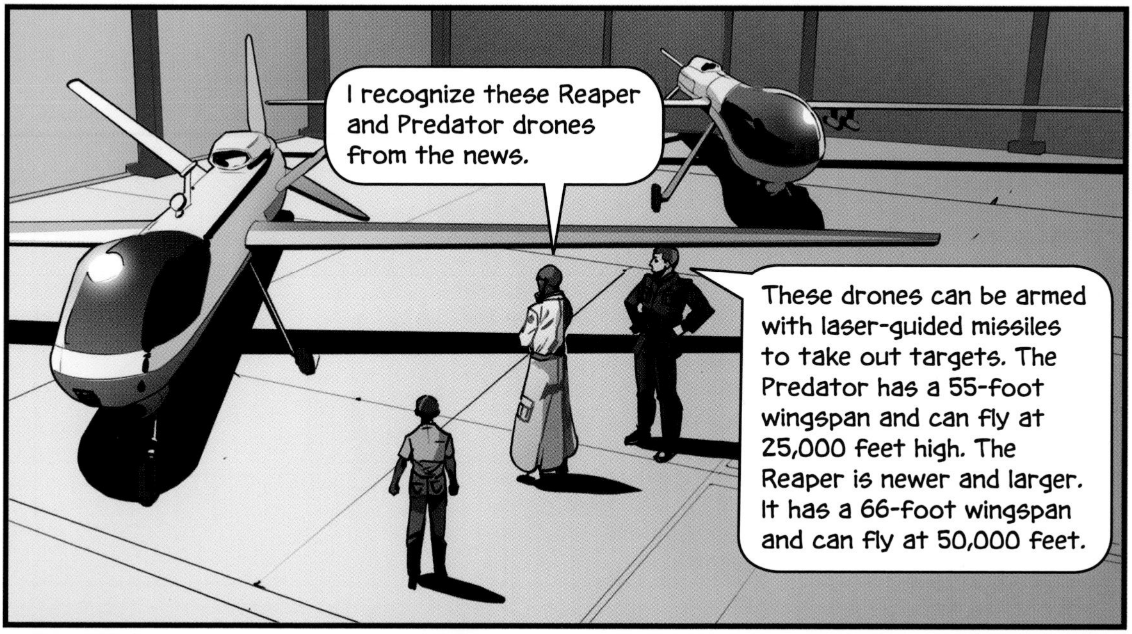
I recognize these Reaper and Predator drones from the news.
These drones can be armed with laser-guided missiles to take out targets. The Predator has a 55-foot wingspan and can fly at 25,000 feet high. The Reaper is newer and larger. It has a 66-foot wingspan and can fly at 50,000 feet.

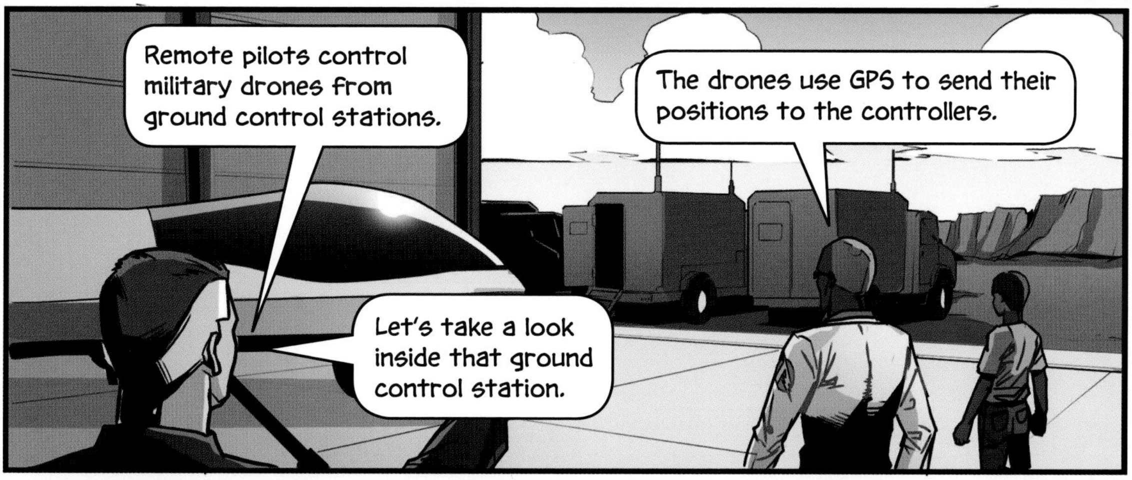
Remote pilots control military drones from ground control stations.
The drones use GPS to send their positions to the controllers.
Let's take a look inside that ground control station.

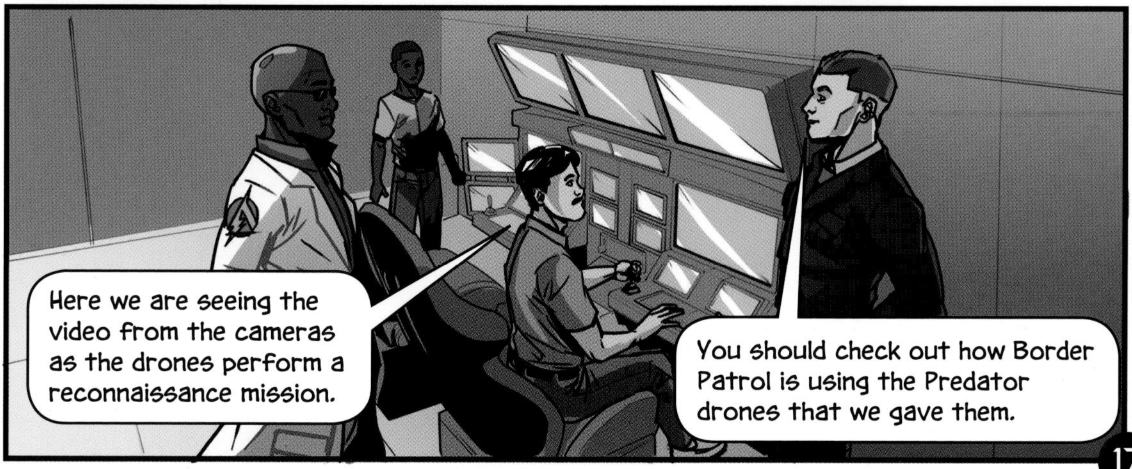
Here we are seeing the video from the cameras as the drones perform a reconnaissance mission.
You should check out how Border Patrol is using the Predator drones that we gave them.

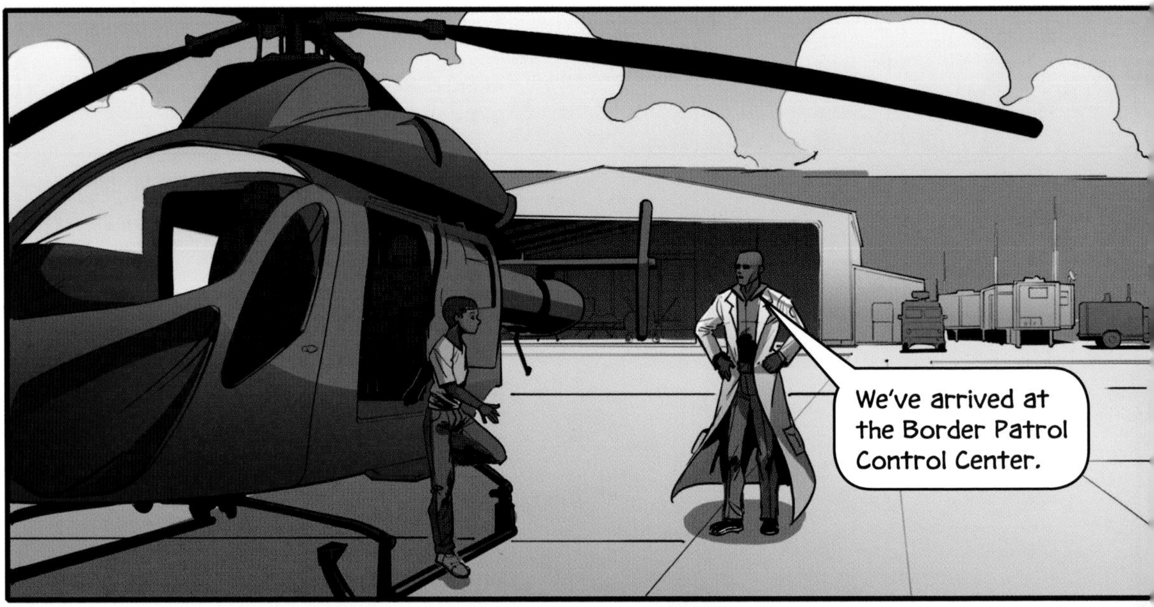
We've arrived at the Border Patrol Control Center.

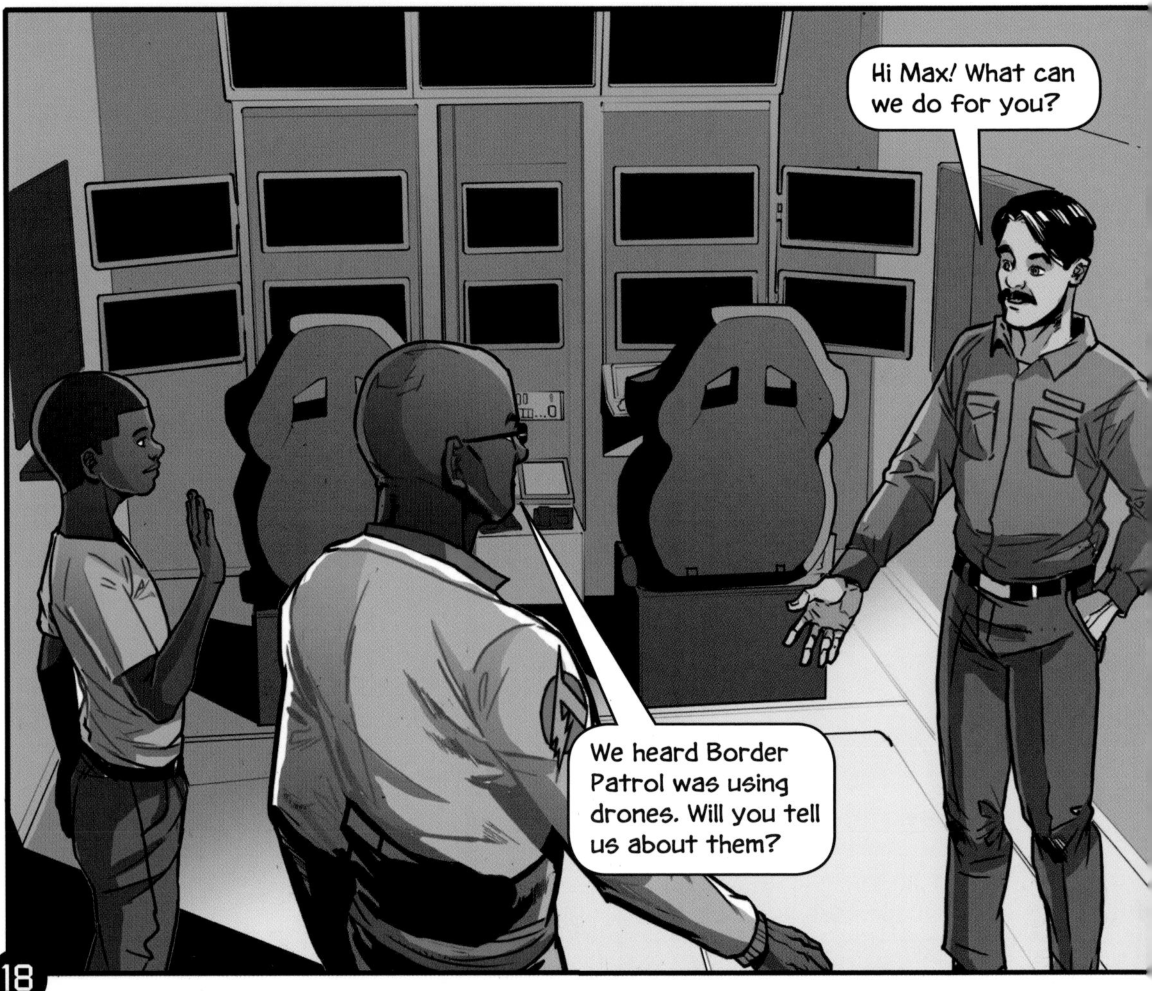
Hi Max! What can we do for you?
We heard Border Patrol was using drones. Will you tell us about them?

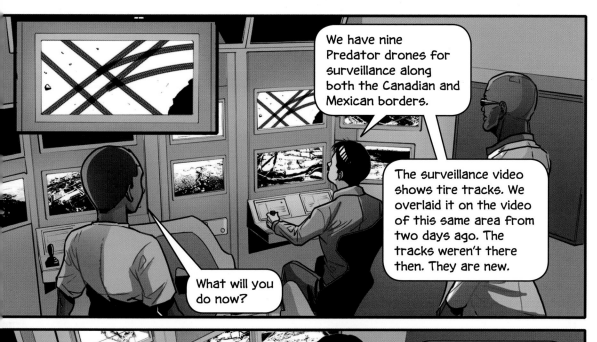

We have nine Predator drones for surveillance along both the Canadian and Mexican borders.

The surveillance video shows tire tracks. We overlaid it on the video of this same area from two days ago. The tracks weren't there then. They are new.

What will you do now?

I am alerting border patrol agents. They will be dispatched to that location to make sure no illegal activities are taking place there.

There are special underwater drones that monitor the ocean borders. Have you seen those yet?

No! Can we, Max?

That will be our next stop.

We're ready to go!

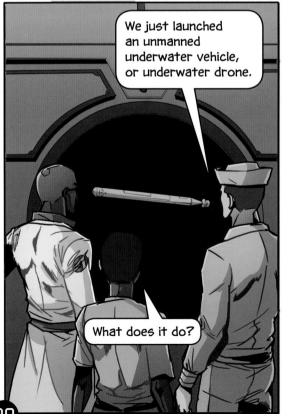

We just launched an unmanned underwater vehicle, or underwater drone.

What does it do?

It detects and removes mines so the submarine can pass safely.

The drone can also listen for other underwater vessels, and send back pictures of the sea floor.

This must be a biomimetic drone. Their designs mimic nature.

Cool!

In March 2011 the Fukushima power plant in Japan was struck by a tsunami triggered by an earthquake. A meltdown of the nuclear reactors released radiation, which made clean-up dangerous. Aerial drones were successfully used to survey the damage and monitor radiation levels. Autonomous drones are also being developed to continually monitor the buildings.

It's our new shark drone. Do you want a demonstration?

You bet!

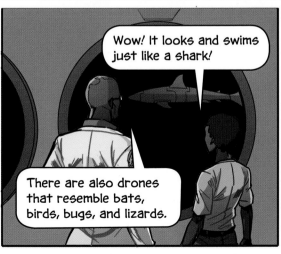

Wow! It looks and swims just like a shark!

There are also drones that resemble bats, birds, bugs, and lizards.

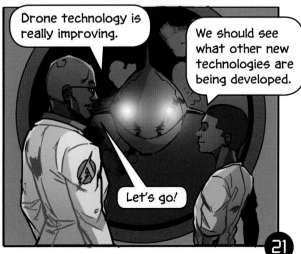

Drone technology is really improving.

We should see what other new technologies are being developed.

Let's go!

21

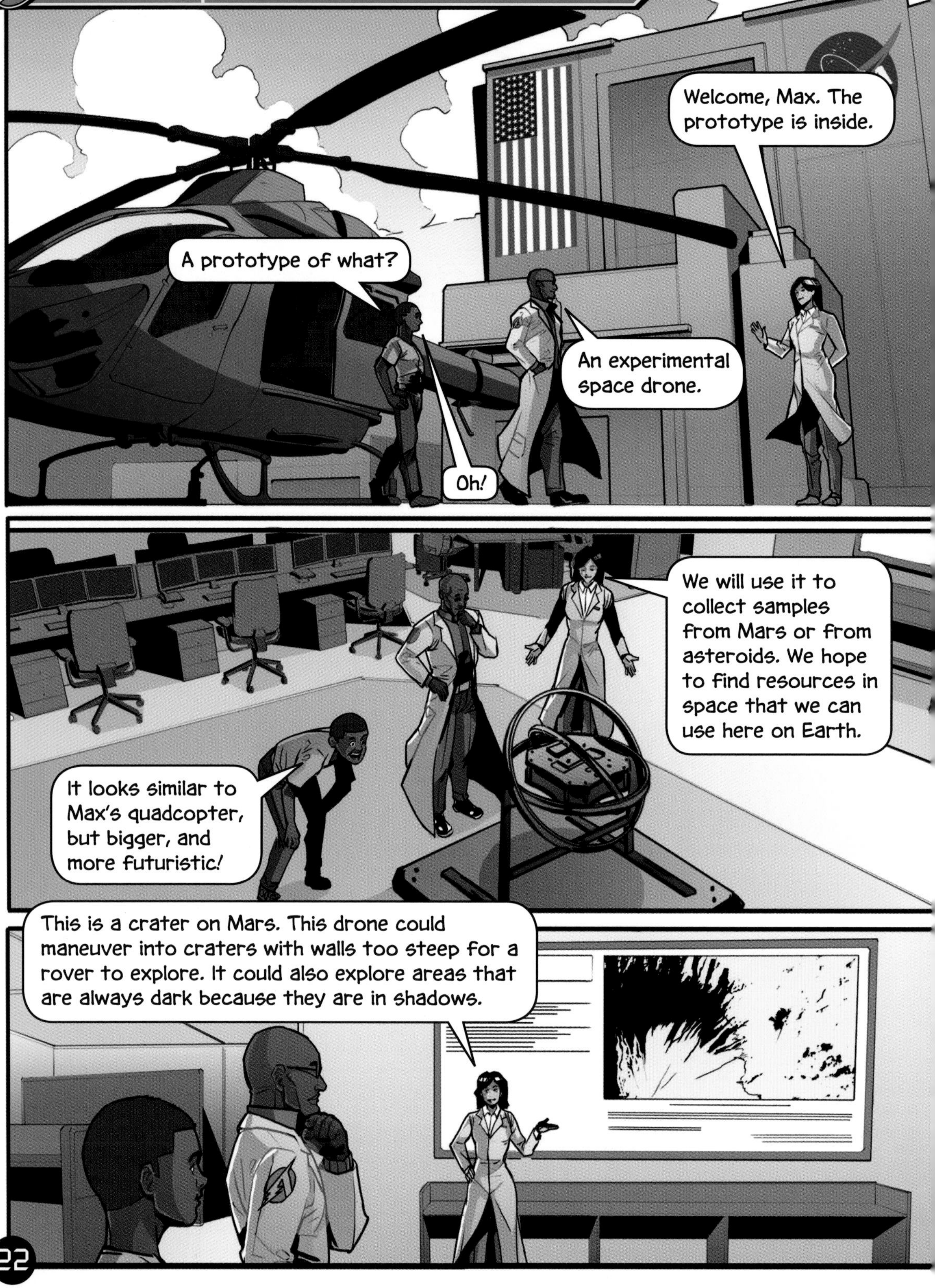
Welcome, Max. The prototype is inside.
A prototype of what?
An experimental space drone.
Oh!
We will use it to collect samples from Mars or from asteroids. We hope to find resources in space that we can use here on Earth.
It looks similar to Max's quadcopter, but bigger, and more futuristic!
This is a crater on Mars. This drone could maneuver into craters with walls too steep for a rover to explore. It could also explore areas that are always dark because they are in shadows.

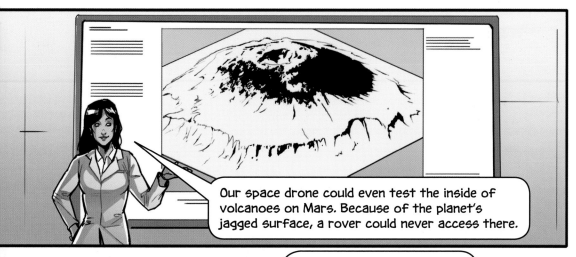

Our space drone could even test the inside of volcanoes on Mars. Because of the planet's jagged surface, a rover could never access there.

I don't see any rotors like on my quadcopter, though.

Rotors push air to move traditional drones around. There is a lack of air in space and in Mars' atmosphere, though, so those rotors wouldn't work there. Instead, cold-gas jets propel the drone in space.

Thanks for showing us your space drone. Do you know of other research showcasing drone technology?

Oh yes! Be sure to check out the experimental solar drones being studied to expand Internet access.

Thanks! We will!

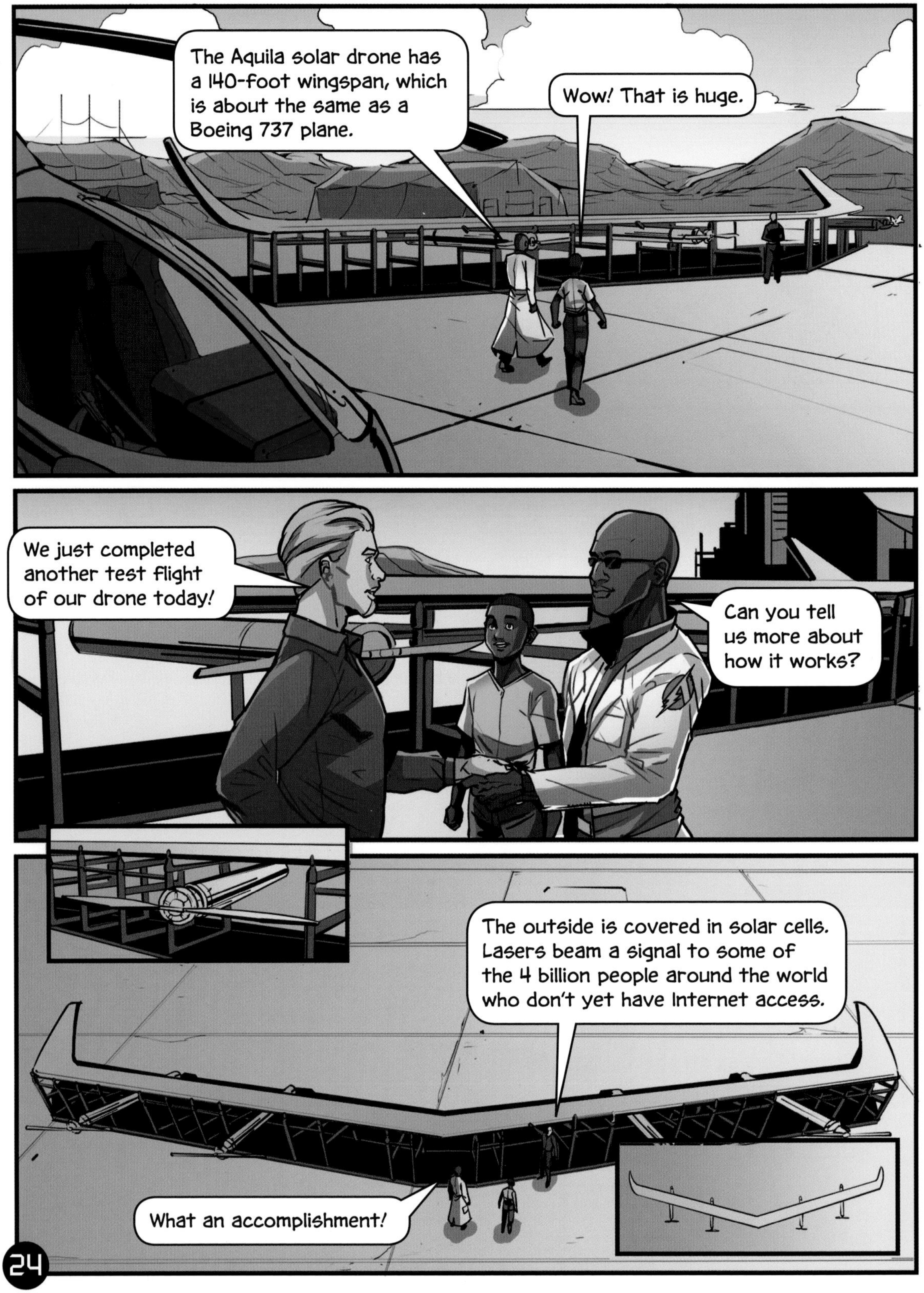
The Aquila solar drone has a 140-foot wingspan, which is about the same as a Boeing 737 plane.
Wow! That is huge.
We just completed another test flight of our drone today!
Can you tell us more about how it works?
The outside is covered in solar cells. Lasers beam a signal to some of the 4 billion people around the world who don't yet have Internet access.
What an accomplishment!

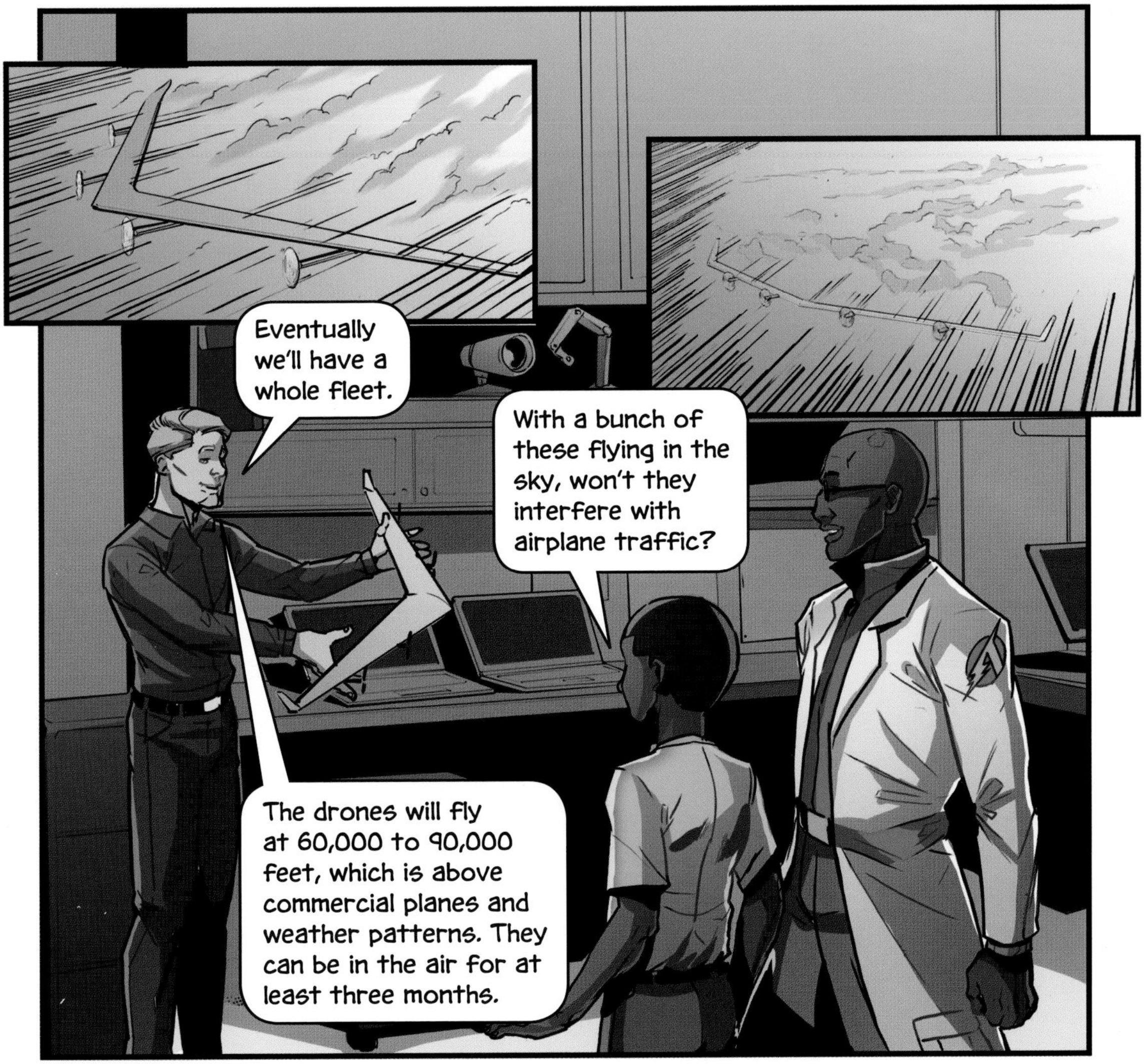
Eventually we'll have a whole fleet.
With a bunch of these flying in the sky, won't they interfere with airplane traffic?
The drones will fly at 60,000 to 90,000 feet, which is above commercial planes and weather patterns. They can be in the air for at least three months.

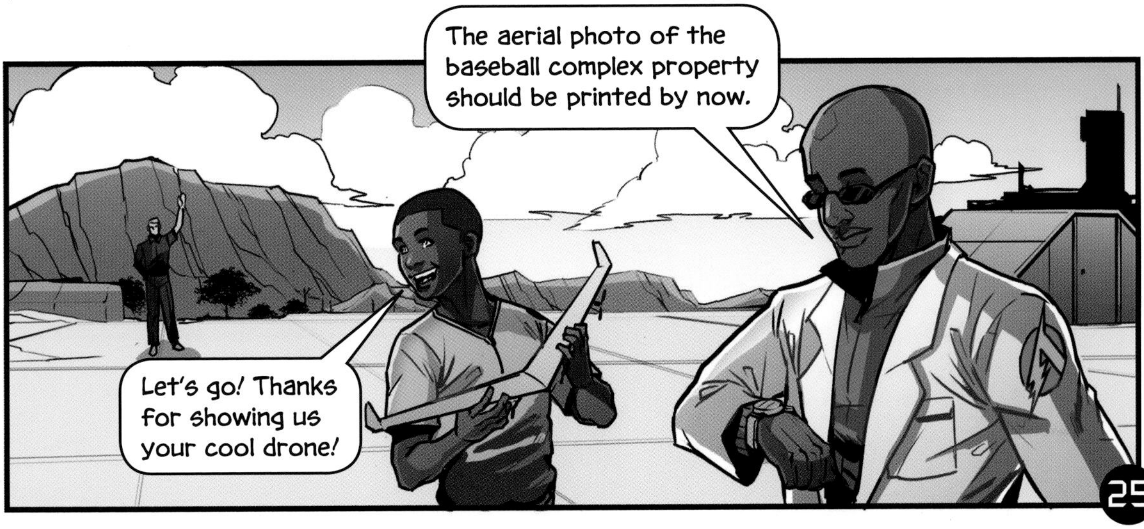
The aerial photo of the baseball complex property should be printed by now.
Let's go! Thanks for showing us your cool drone!

The photo shop is right around the corner. We can walk if you want more practice flying my drone.

Sure!

In the future, the photo shop may be able to deliver aerial photos directly to the city by drone.

Really?

Some online companies are already testing drone delivery for lightweight packages.

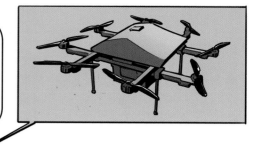

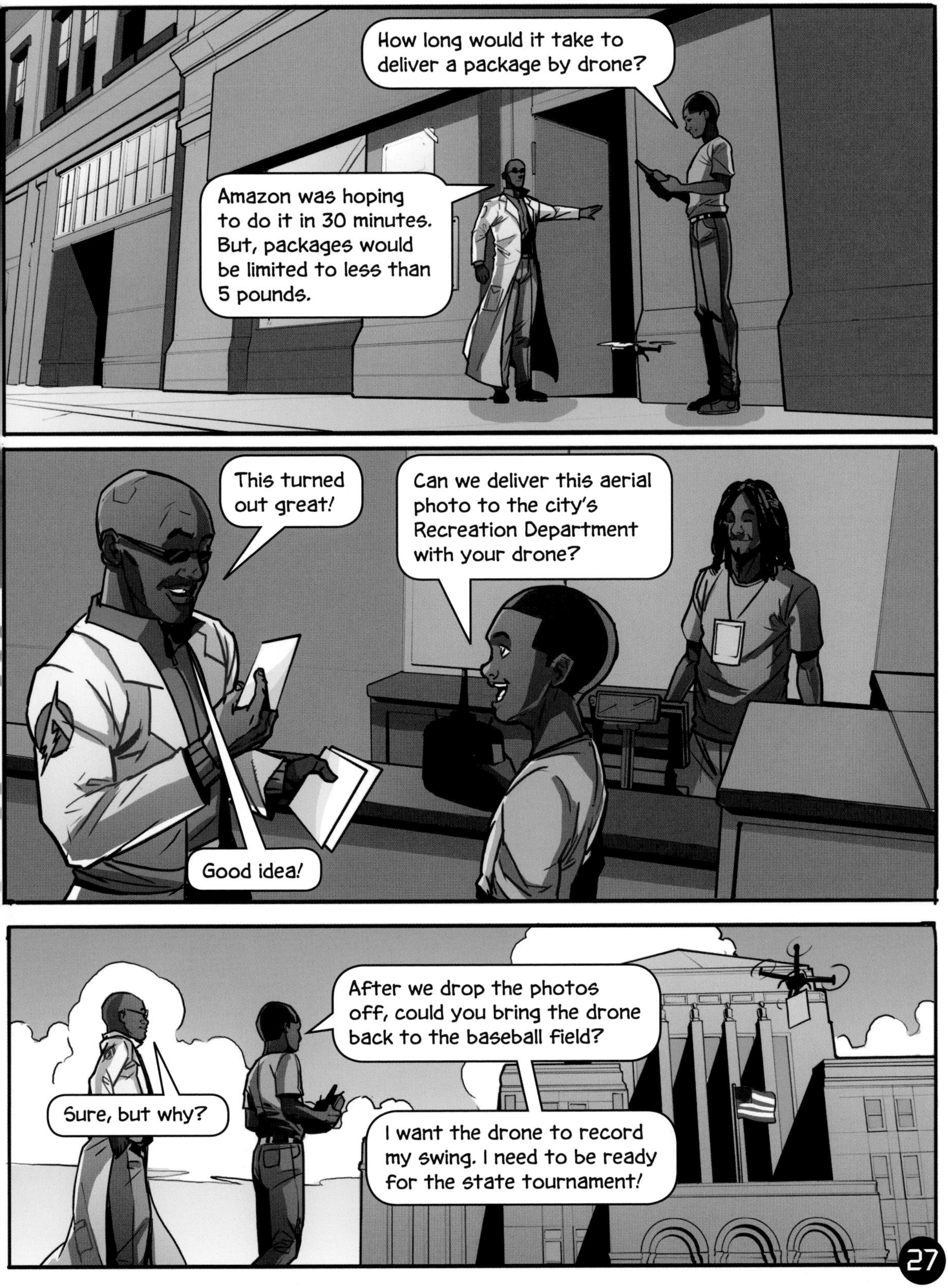
How long would it take to deliver a package by drone?
Amazon was hoping to do it in 30 minutes. But, packages would be limited to less than 5 pounds.
This turned out great!
Can we deliver this aerial photo to the city's Recreation Department with your drone?
Good idea!
After we drop the photos off, could you bring the drone back to the baseball field?
Sure, but why?
I want the drone to record my swing. I need to be ready for the state tournament!

MORE ABOUT
DRONES

Radio-controlled and remote-controlled planes were experimented with as far back as World War I (1914–1918).

The first drone as we know it was built by engineer Abraham Karem in the early 1980s. His drone, known as the Albatross, could fly for as long as 56 hours. His design led to the development of the Predator drone.

On December 1, 2013, Amazon unveiled its plan to explore drone package delivery.

In Rwanda, Africa, life-saving drones are delivering blood and medical supplies to clinics.

The United States Navy uses drones on their ships. Aerial drones can locate and follow smuggler's ships for miles without being noticed.

Between 2 and 3 million drones were sold to American consumers in 2016 alone. More than 9 million drones were purchased around the world.

On October 7, 2001, the first Predator drones to be armed with missiles began missions over Afghanistan after the September 11, 2001 attacks in the US.

In 2017, Super Bowl 51 featured a halftime show with 300 syncronized Shooting Star drones. The quadcopters were outfitted with LED lights. A single operator controlled all the drones.

CRITICAL THINKING QUESTIONS

1. Taking aerial photographs can be fun. But one quick photo of a person — or their property — can lead to ethical issues. How might drone technology interfere with peoples' privacy?

2. Drones have been used to film movies, deliver pizza, and hunt hurricanes. How might drones continue to help people in their everyday lives?

3. People who operate small drones for fun do not need a permit or special paperwork to fly. What kinds of problems might this cause? Do you think all drone pilots should have a license?

MORE ABOUT

MAX AXIOM
SUPER SCIENTIST

Real name: Maxwell J. Axiom
Hometown: Seattle, Washington
Height: 6' 1" Weight: 192 lbs
Eyes: Brown Hair: None

Super capabilities: Super intelligence; able to shrink to the size of an atom; sunglasses give x-ray vision; lab coat allows for travel through time and space.

Origin: Since birth, Max Axiom seemed destined for greatness. His mother, a marine biologist, taught her son about the mysteries of the sea. His father, a nuclear physicist and volunteer park ranger, schooled Max on the wonders of earth and sky.

One day on a wilderness hike, a megacharged lightning bolt struck Max with blinding fury. When he awoke, Max discovered a newfound energy and set out to learn as much about science as possible. He traveled the globe earning degrees in every aspect of the field. Upon his return, he was ready to share his knowledge and new identity with the world. He had become Max Axiom, Super Scientist.

GLOSSARY

aerial (AYR-ee-uhl)—relating to something that happens in the skies

autonomous (aw-TAH-nuh-muhss)—able to control oneself; autonomous robots are not operated remotely by a person

biomimetic (BY-oh-mi-MET-ik)—imitating the design of a living thing

Global Positioning System (GLOH-buhl puh-ZI-shuh-ning SISS-tuhm)—an electronic tool used to find the location of an object; this system is often called GPS

infrared (in-fruh-RED)—light waves in the electromagnetic spectrum between visible light and microwaves

irrigate (IHR-uh-gate)—to supply water for crops

pitch (PICH)—the angle of the blades on an aircraft; pitch determines whether an aircraft moves up or down

reconnaissance (ree-KAH-nuh-suhnss)—a mission to gather information about an enemy

rotor (ROH-tur)—the system of rotating blades on a helicopter; a rotor provides force to lift a helicopter or drone into the air

satellite (SAT-uh-lite)—a spacecraft used to send signals and information from one place to another

surveillance (suhr-VAY-luhnss)—the act of keeping very close watch on someone, someplace, or something

throttle (THROT-uhl)—a lever, pedal, or handle used to control the speed of an engine

READ MORE

d, Douglas. *Discover Drones*. Searchlight Books:
's Cool About Science? Minneapolis: Lerner
cations, 2017.

sico, Katie. *Drones*. A True Book. New York:
ildren's Press, an imprint of Scholastic Inc., 2016.

Newman, Lauren. *Drones*. 21st Century Skills Innovation
Library: Emerging Tech. Ann Arbor, Mich.: Cherry Lake
Publishing, 2018.

Olson, Elsie. *Drones*. Modern Engineering Marvels.
Minneapolis: Abdo Pub., 2017.

INTERNET SITES

Use FactHound to find Internet sites related to this book.

Visit *www.facthound.com*

Just type in 9781515773900 and go.

Super-cool stuff!

Check out projects, games and lots more at
www.capstonekids.com

Index

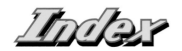